COLORADO

Photographs by

STEVE TOHARI

SHETLAND PRESS • Breckenridge, Colorado

©1997 SHETLAND PRESS
All Photographs ©Steve Tohari

Design by Steve Tohari
Text by Steve Tohari
Photo Editing by Steve Tohari
Type by Martha Bird
Encouragement by Pam Demma

SHETLAND PRESS
P.O. Box 5347
Breckenridge, Colorado 80424

Printed and Bound in HONG KONG

ISBN#0-9657504-1-8 (hard cover)
ISBN#0-9657504-0-X (soft cover)

PREFACE

The color photographs on the following pages represent a small sample from my extensive portfolio. All the images have been hand-printed, framed, and sold many times over a period of fourteen years.

The color reproductions in this book have been made directly from my hand-made color-corrected color *prints* instead of from uncorrected color *slides* as is customary in the production of photographic books. The result is superior color rendition and contrast control.

No attempt has been made to arrange the images by season or area. As you flip the pages, you will want to focus on each image individually.

This book is not a lengthy documentary on Colorado - it is a collection of my impressions, an attempt to convey not just a pretty place, but a deeper state of mind.

STEVE TOHARI / Photographer - Photo Lab Technician   28 February 1997 - Breckenridge, Colorado

Aspen - Golden Gate State Park above Golden

Hallett Peak - Rocky Mountain National Park

Fall River - Rocky Mountain National Park

September Snow - Breckenridge

Buck - Great Sand Dunes National Monument

Wildflowers near Vail Pass

Autumn Leaves - Maroon Bells near Aspen

Blue Lake - San Juan Mountains near Ouray

Pyramid Peak and Maroon Bells from Aspen Highlands

Aspen Grove - Elk Creek near Steamboat Springs

Castle Peak - Pearl Pass above Aspen

The Outback at Keystone

Wildflowers - Elk Range near Marble

Dead Horse Mill near Marble

Fog - Storm Peak, Steamboat

Primrose - Porphiry Basin above Telluride

Sunrise - Maroon Bells above Aspen

Street Lights at dawn - Breckenridge

Ten Mile Range from Copper Mountain

Last Dollar Road near Telluride

Aspen leaves above Breckenridge

Reflections - Maroon Lake above Aspen

Aspen - Ten Mile Range near Breckenridge

Trappers Lake - Flattops Range near Yampa

Hoarfrost near Breckenridge

Ancient Bristlecone Pine - Mt. Evans

Autumn - Cascades near Vail

Old Barn - Steamboat

Aspen - Mt. Wilson near Telluride

Wildflowers near Crested Butte

Aspen at Beaver Creek

Black Canyon of the Gunnison

Breckenridge from Keystone

Town of Breckenridge

Sunset - Molas Lake above Silverton

Sunset - Colorado National Monument near Grand Junction

Rocky Mountain Columbine above Silverton

Wildflowers, Cascades near Montezuma

Aspen on Boreas Pass above Breckenridge

Gore Range above Silverthorne

Rocky Mountain Wildflowers

Columbine - Mt. Neva above Eldora

San Juan Mountains near Ouray

Lodgepole Pines - Genesee

Old Barn - Aspen near Telluride

Buffalo in Snowstorm - Genesee

Gilpin Lake - Zirkel Range near Steamboat Springs

Autumn - Maroon Lake above Aspen

Old Wagon near Breckenridge

Wildflowers, Tarn - Mt. Neva above Eldora

Near Capitol Peak above Snowmass

Maroon Bells - Aspen

Ferns, Aspen - near Crested Butte

Sunset from the summit of Mt. Evans

Juniper, Cliff Dwellings - Mesa Verde National Park

Aspen - Dallas Divide / San Juan Mountains

Wildflowers - Shrine Ridge above Vail Pass

Mt. Wilson near Telluride

Back Bowls - Vail

Coney Flats above Boulder

Ancient Bristlecone Pine - Mt. Evans

Aspen Road near Crystal City

Hagerman Peak above Snowmass

Moonlight on Aspen

Old Cabin near Breckenridge

Ten Mile Range from Boreas Pass

Gore Range from Shrine Ridge above Vail Pass

Yankee Boy Basin above Ouray

Spring - Maroon Bells above Aspen

Rifle Falls near Rifle

Flatirons - Boulder

Sunset - Great Sand Dunes National Monument

Wildflowers, Gore Range

Aspen Leaves - First Snow, Ten Mile Range

Sapphire Point - Lake Dillon

Wildflowers - Yankee Boy Basin above Ouray

Reflections, San Juan Mountains

Sunset - Peak 8, Breckenridge

Capitol Peak above Snowmass

Dallas Divide - San Juan Mountains

Columbine - Ice Lake above Silverton

Aspen Leaves - Pond near Telluride

Silver Creek Pass above Crystal City

Bridal Veil Falls - Telluride

American Basin near Lake City

Elk, Long's Peak - Rocky Mountain National Park

Columbine - Yankee Boy Basin above Ouray

Primrose - Gore Range

Garden of the Gods, Pike's Peak - Colorado Springs

Aspen - Lake Dillon

Beaver Pond - Clear Creek near Vicksburg

PHOTOGRAPHER'S NOTES

Cameras:	MAMIYA RB-67 Pro-S ($2^{1}/_{4}$" x $2^{3}/_{4}$" negative size)
	PENTAX 645 ($1^{5}/_{8}$" x $2^{1}/_{4}$" negative size)
	FUJICA 645-S ($1^{5}/_{8}$" x $2^{1}/_{4}$" negative size)
Film:	KODAK Kodacolor VR Gold ASA 100 / 120 Roll Size
Paper:	KODAK Supra / RA N-surface (for reproduction)
Print Processor:	KREONITE 26" Roller Transport

Sunset - Breckenridge